Need to Know
Eating
Disorders

Caroline Warbrick

H

www.heinemann.co.uk

visit our website to find out more information about **Heinemann Library** books.

To order:

☎ Phone 44 (0) 1865 888066

🖹 Send a fax to 44 (0) 1865 314091

💻 Visit the Heinemann Bookshop at www.heinemann.co.uk to browse our catalogue and order online.

First published in Great Britain by Heinemann Library, Halley Court, Jordan Hill, Oxford OX2 8EJ,
part of Harcourt Education.
Heinemann is a registered trademark of Harcourt Education Ltd.

© Harcourt Education Ltd 2002.
First published in paperback in 2003
The moral right of the proprietor has been asserted.

Designed by M2 Graphic Design
Originated by Ambassador Litho Ltd.
Printed in China by South China Printers

ISBN 0431 097992 (hardback)   ISBN 0431 098069 (paperback)

06 05 04 03   07 06 05 04 03
10 9 8 7 6 5 4 3 2   10 9 8 7 6 5 4 3 2 1

British Library Cataloguing in Publication Data
Warbrick, Caroline
Eating disorders.-(Need to know)
1.Eating disorders - Juvenile literature
I.Title
362.1'9'68526

Acknowledgements
The Publishers would like to thank the following for permission to reproduce photographs:
Bubbles pp12, 14 (David Robinson), 41 (Chris Rout), 44, 45, Camera Press London pp 7, 11, 13,
Capital pictures p38, Corbis p23, 47 (top) (Layne Kennedy), Getty Images (Zigy Katuzny) p49,
Images colour library pp5, 47 (bottom), Mary Evans Picture Library p35, Popperfoto p21, Powerstock
Zefa p9, Rhodes Farm Clinic p27, Robert Harding Picture Library p28, Science Photo Library p48, 53,
Stone pp15, 17, 19, 25, 29, 31, 32, 33, 43, The Stock Market pp37, 51.

Cover photograph reproduced with permission of Telegraph Colour Library.

The publishers would like to thank Bridget Lawless for her assistance in the preparation of this book.

Every effort has been made to contact copyright holders of any material reproduced in this book. Any omis-
sions will be rectified in subsequent printings if notice is given to the publisher.

Contents

Any words appearing in the text in bold, **like this**, are explained in the Glossary.

Eating disorders

When Nikki Hughes died of starvation at the age of 23 she weighed just 30kg (4st 11lb). Nikki died after an 8 year struggle with the **eating disorder**, **anorexia** nervosa which locked her into a battle with food and her body.

Nikki was 16 when she first became concerned about her weight. She started to diet, cutting back on food whenever she could. Often her meals would consist solely of a slice of tomato and a slice of pepper. By the time she died, Nikki was living on just sips of water. Nikki's sister remembers: 'I saw her getting thinner and thinner. I remember the shock of realizing what had happened the day my mother carried her upstairs like a baby. She looked just like the pictures you see on television of people in famines, starving to death. She was so thin but she still saw herself as a size 20.'

Nikki's story is not an isolated case. In the UK it is estimated that 1 in 25 women aged between 15 and 35 have an eating disorder. The figures for the USA are similar. Men are also affected, and the Eating Disorders Association currently estimate that approximately 10 per cent of people with eating disorders are men.

Big news

Eating disorders are such big news it may make you wonder if it is normal to have one! Every week we seem to hear of someone's battle with anorexia, **bulimia** or **bingeing**. Newspapers love to speculate about whether a celebrity has an eating disorder and we like to read such stories. There are talk shows on television devoted to people's agonies with their weight and eating habits. Problem pages in magazines are full of people's misery as they fight with secret bingeing, **obsessions** with food, hatred of their body and punishing diets and exercise schedules.

Is there a difference between having an eating disorder and the day-to-day concerns that people have about their diet, weight and body? Is feeling dissatisfied with your body, going on a diet or thinking carefully about what you eat necessarily a problem? Or is it the beginning of the slippery slope down into eating disorders and illness? This book will help to make clear what eating disorders are. It will explain how professionals describe eating disorders, and the signs they look for to decide if someone has an illness. It will also explain why some people develop eating disorders and suggest ways of coping with these illnesses.

What are eating disorders?

An **eating disorder** is the name given to a range of problems that people have with eating and the way they think and feel about their bodies. Some of these problems are caused by people eating too little, and others by eating too much. Other eating disorders are caused by the things people do to keep their weight down.

There are three main types of eating disorders: **anorexia** nervosa, **bulimia** nervosa and **compulsive** eating disorder (also known as binge eating disorder). Those who suffer from anorexia nervosa, or anorexia, are known as anorexics. Sufferers of bulimia nervosa are called bulimics.

Anorexia is characterized by deliberate attempts to lose weight by the individual. It is likely to be the condition that comes most readily to mind when people are asked to talk about eating disorders. Most people are able to describe some of its symptoms – for example, excessive dieting, extreme thinness and a **distorted** body image.

Bulimics experience episodes of uncontrollable eating, called **bingeing**, followed by periods of **purging**. Purging is where the bulimic attempts to get rid of all the food they have eaten by either making themselves sick or by taking **laxatives**.

People with compulsive eating disorders also find it hard to stop eating or thinking about food. However, unlike bulimics, they do not engage in purging. Many people with compulsive eating disorders also have problems with being overweight.

What are eating disorders?

Eating disorders:
- are not primarily about food but about underlying emotional turmoil
- include anorexia nervosa, bulimia nervosa, and compulsive eating disorder
- can affect women and men of all ages, from all backgrounds and ethnic groups.

Eating disorders are not just about food, but underlying emotional turmoil.

What are eating disorders?

Recognizing the signs

Often doctors and other professionals have to decide whether someone has an eating disorder. They look for a number of signs and then try to make judgements about how much of a problem these things are for the person. Some of the signs are easy to recognize, for example, the physical **symptoms** that are a direct result of some eating disorders. Other signs are much harder to detect, for example, the way someone feels and thinks about themselves and how they behave around food. It is relatively easy to tell when someone has extreme problems. However, it is much more difficult to make judgements about thinking, feelings and behaviour which are only slightly different from normal. Here are some of the things professionals might look for as clues of eating disorders:

Physical symptoms

Excessive dieting, **bingeing** and **purging** all cause physical changes in the body. These are relatively easy for a doctor to detect and are discussed in more detail later in the book.

Feelings

Eating disorders are not primarily about food, they are about underlying emotional **distress**. Very often people with eating disorders feel deeply unhappy and are in considerable distress about themselves and their eating habits. They talk about feeling ugly and hating themselves. They also feel a lot of guilt, **anxiety** and fear about their eating and their bodies. They often feel out of control, particularly around food.

Thoughts

People with eating disorders are often troubled by **obsessive** thoughts about food, their weight and their bodies. Often these thoughts are very negative. For example, an anorexic might be troubled by how many **calories** they have eaten. Or, if they haven't managed to exercise, how much weight they might have put on in a day. Bulimics might not be able to get out of their mind their walk home past a cake shop. Often people with eating disorders think about themselves in **distorted** ways.

For example, anorexics often see themselves as fat even though they are very thin.

Behaviour

Many people with eating disorders often behave in odd ways, particularly around food. For example, an anorexic might show a great interest in food – preparing and serving it for others – but then refuse to eat it themselves. People suffering from **bulimia** might always avoid other people after eating. Or they might have certain times in the day when they are very angry about being disturbed. This is because they want to make themselves sick in secret.

People with eating disorders do not fit into neat categories. However, there are some useful guidelines to help professionals decide whether someone is experiencing problems:

People with **compulsive** eating disorders or bulimia may:
- overeat in secret, either all or some of the time
- feel guilty that their eating is not normal
- feel guilty about what they have eaten and feel like a bad person
- try constantly to lose weight but fail in their attempts

- think about food much of the time
- feel out of control around certain kinds of food or any food
- make themselves vomit or take **laxatives** to get rid of unwanted food.

People with **anorexia** may:
- be underweight but feel overweight
- be terrified of gaining weight
- be very fearful of eating
- eat extremely little food or only a few types of foods
- exercise excessively.

Anorexia nervosa

Anorexia nervosa is the best known **eating disorder**. Most people are able to describe some of its **symptoms** – for example, excessive dieting, extreme weight loss and fear of food.

'Anorexia nervosa' literally means 'loss of appetite for nervous reason'. However, this definition is slightly misleading because the sufferer has, in fact, not lost their appetite. Anorexics often feel extremely hungry and think about food all the time. They do not allow themselves to eat because they are afraid of what the food will do to them, or are disgusted by the act of eating itself. People with anorexia try to avoid eating by avoiding food altogether, or by reducing their **calorie** intake. They may also get rid of calories eaten by exercising excessively or **purging**. Some anorexics restrict, to a dangerous level, the amounts they eat and drink.

❝Sometimes there were days I would eat hardly anything at all. Even so, every morning I would get up early so that I could cycle to the local pool and do lengths before school.❞

(Maria 15)

The deeper problem

Anorexics devote so much energy to food that it is hard to realize that anorexia is not really about food at all. In fact, the roots of anorexia lie in deep unhappiness, anxiety and low **self-esteem**. These feelings lead the anorexic to develop ways of behaving that help them to feel better about themselves and more in control. However, since this behaviour does not solve their problems, the anorexic is locked into a continuing battle, with very negative effects.

What are the signs?

When deciding if someone has anorexia nervosa, professionals look for signs or symptoms in the body, the mind and the behaviour of the person.

The physical symptoms of anorexia result from the effects of **starvation** on the body. There is lowered resistance to illnesses, physical weakness and extreme weight loss. Many anorexics suffer from dizzy spells and fainting and women stop having monthly periods. **Constipation** and abdominal pain are also very common, as are a swollen stomach, face and ankles, downy hair on the body, poor blood circulation and feeling cold. In the long-term anorexics run the risk of losing some of their bone mass and may eventually suffer from **osteoporosis**, or brittle bones. Some women who recover from anorexia find it difficult to become pregnant in later life.

Anorexia nervosa

Many anorexics think about themselves in distinctive ways. For example, they have an intense fear of gaining weight, and often have a very **distorted** picture of their body shape and weight. Anorexics see themselves as fat although they are extremely thin. **Depression** and unhappiness are very common feelings in people with this **eating disorder**.

Often when people develop **anorexia** they show distinct changes in the way they behave. A person may change from being focused and clear-minded, to being indecisive and having problems concentrating. Often anorexics behave in strange ways around food. They may be anxious to cook for others but unwilling to eat themselves. Sometimes they develop **rituals** when preparing or eating food – eating very slowly or only off 'their own plate'. Anorexics often change the way they dress – wearing large sweaters and baggy clothes to disguise their thinness. It is also likely that a previously sociable person will start to become withdrawn.

❝Both my family and friends would question me endlessly on why I was not eating. Was I ill, worried about my exams? They also noticed that I was always cold. Even in the middle of summer I would be wearing a big sweatshirt. Eventually my mum made me go to the doctors.❞

(Julie 15)

Jenny

Jenny had always been popular and successful at school. She was good at most subjects but had a special talent for music. At the age of 14 Jenny was asked to play in a school concert. The next day one of the boys in her class made a nasty comment about her weight. Although Jenny knew the boy was trying to be funny in front of his friends, she took the comment to heart and decided to go on a diet.

Jenny became **obsessed** by her diet and losing weight. There were days when she hardly ate anything at all. Jenny also started to spend a lot more time on her own in her room, studying or practising, and no longer wanted to go out with her friends. Everyone noticed a gradual change in Jenny. Besides losing weight they also saw her becoming more introverted and unhappy. She seemed to lack the enthusiasm and energy she had shown when she was younger. Jenny's mother eventually persuaded her to visit the doctor. At the time her weight was below 6 stones (41kg). She was diagnosed as anorexic.

Both dancers and models are under pressure to maintain ultra-thin bodies required for their professions.

Bulimia

It is only in the last 30 years that **bulimia** nervosa has been recognized by doctors as an **eating disorder** in its own right. Professionals involved in the study of eating disorders noticed that there were significant numbers of people who were not **anorexic** but still had problems with eating and their weight. However, instead of starving themselves these people admitted to hating their bodies and weight yet regularly, and often secretly, eating large quantities of food. Then, unable to stop eating even when physically full, they would attempt to control their weight by making themselves vomit, by crash dieting or by using **laxatives**. Most of these people were disgusted by their behaviour and aware that it could not be normal. However, they were unable to overcome their need to eat and then get rid of the food. At first bulimia was thought to be a rare disorder. Now recent studies show that it is strikingly common among young women.

Binge eating

The term bulimia is used to describe an illness that contains a range of very specific behaviours. Bulimics have regular episodes of binge eating, usually in private. Foods eaten during a binge often include biscuits, chocolate, crisps, bowls of cereal, large amounts of toast with butter, cakes and ice cream.

Sometimes the food is enjoyed, but it is more likely to be eaten quickly and without really tasting. Often this kind of eating will be accompanied by feelings of **anxiety**, guilt and **remorse**. Following a binge, but not always immediately afterwards, bulimics attempt to get rid of the food they have eaten. They do this by making themselves sick, and/or by taking laxatives. Some bulimics try to compensate for a binge by excessively exercising or by crash dieting.

The characteristic cycle of **bingeing** and **purging** can vary from person to person. Some people binge and purge several times a day, and others only once or twice a month. The average is once daily, with the number of **calories** consumed in the binge ranging from 1200 to 11,500. This compares to an average intake for a healthy young woman of around 2000 calories during the course of a whole day.

STYLE

Bulimia

Like **anorexia** nervosa, the roots of **bulimia** lie in the way people feel about themselves. Their attitude to food is a **symptom** of unhappiness, for example, not of a dislike of food.

The difficult thing about bulimia is that once someone gets into the cycle of **bingeing** and **purging** it is very hard to break. Purging causes the person to become hungry which in turns triggers thoughts of food and eating. This thinking about food becomes obsessional and continues until the bulimic starts to eat again, often uncontrollably. Driven by thoughts of guilt, disgust and self-loathing the person purges themselves of all they have eaten and the cycle begins again.

What are the signs?

Bulimia is far harder to detect than anorexia. Bulimics are often of normal weight and usually take great care to make sure that their illness is kept a secret. However, there are some signs that suggest someone might be experiencing problems.

If someone has been suffering from bulimia for some time there can be physical changes in the body, some of which can be quite dangerous. Many of these changes are caused by excessive vomiting and **laxative** use. Regular vomiting can lead to a sore throat, erosion of the teeth, swollen **salivary glands** and poor skin condition. It can also upset the body's fluid and mineral balance. Lower amounts of potassium in the body can lead to muscle cramps and weakness, kidney damage and irregular heartbeat. There is also a possibility of irregular periods, tiredness and general lack of energy. Through binge eating, the stomach can become swollen and sometimes painful. Laxatives can lead to **dehydration** and **constipation** and, with long term use, the possibility of **incontinence**. However, once cured of bulimia the individual returns to normal, relatively quickly.

Bulimia is very distressing for the sufferer. The bulimic is obsessed by thoughts of food and eating. However, after eating they feel disgust and self-loathing and are driven to rid themselves of food.

Bulimia

Bulimics also show **distorted** patterns of thinking and feeling. Typically bulimics have an **obsession** with food and experience uncontrollable urges to eat vast amounts of food. Like anorexics they have distorted perceptions about their weight and shape, and are often desperately unhappy about themselves and their behaviour. Bulimics talk about loathing themselves and their bodies.

Bulimics often behave in strange ways. One of the surest signs that someone is bulimic is if they always avoid other people after eating, usually they will have gone to the bathroom to vomit.

Bulimics sometimes stay awake late into the night and become very irritable if they are disturbed. These can be signs that they are secretly **bingeing**. Like anorexics, bulimics may have periods of **fasting** and excessive exercise. Some bulimics may also have other behavioural problems such as stealing money, shoplifting for food or intentionally hurting themselves.

❝I fantasize about all the food I'd most like to eat and then go off on a spending spree. At home I lay it all out in a particular manner, almost as if I'm going to entertain, and then plough my way through the whole lot. Then I'm horrified at the sight of my painfully overstuffed stomach and feel like the nearest thing to a human pig.❞

(Clare 16)

From an early age, food can be seen as a reward or something that makes us feel better. Comfort eating can turn to feelings of disgust and remorse for a bulimic though.

Compulsive eating disorder

Like **bulimia**, **compulsive eating disorder** (also known as binge eating disorder) has only recently been recognized as a distinct condition. The two disorders share many common features, such as overeating, guilt and **remorse** about **bingeing** and self-loathing. Compulsive eaters differ from bulimics in that after a bingeing session they do not try to rid themselves of the food they have consumed. As a result, many compulsive eaters are likely to be overweight and, in 10 per cent of cases, **obese**.

It is thought that many more people suffer from compulsive eating disorder than either **anorexia** or bulimia. However, fewer people are coming forward for help. A number of reasons might be behind this. Many people have times when they overeat – just think about Christmas! – and others admit to thinking about food a lot. Struggles with eating and dieting seem part of everyday life. It is possible that some people who have serious problems with their eating do not see themselves as needing professional help. They think of themselves as 'weak-willed' and needing to try harder when they diet! Other people might be afraid of coming forward for help because of the **stigma** of being overweight and overeating. Finally, there are people who really don't see themselves as having a problem. They just like food and don't mind being overweight.

Health risks

Compulsive eating disorder affects men and women of all ages, but it is mostly women who seek help. Some of the main concerns over this eating disorder are related to the effects that being overweight has on health. Experts generally agree that there are health risks when someone becomes more than 30lb (13kg) overweight. They are more likely to be at risk of high blood pressure, heart disease, diabetes and certain types of cancer.

What are the signs?

People with compulsive eating disorder behave in a number of distinct ways. When having a meal they often eat very rapidly. They frequently eat large amounts of food when they are not hungry. This can be by continuous eating, or 'grazing', throughout the day or by having binges of large amounts of food.Often bingeing takes place in secret. However the eating occurs, the person often feels guilty about overeating and has feelings of self-loathing. Compulsive eaters often describe feeling very lonely and **depressed**.

For many people with compulsive eating disorder food is a source of comfort. Often they feel very sad or lonely and eat to make themselves feel better.

Compulsive eating disorder

Many **compulsive** eaters are 'always on a diet' – watching what they eat or how much they weigh. They make great efforts to lose weight, including starving, exercising excessively and spending a lot on diet books and low-**calorie** food. However, very often these efforts are finished by a small setback that then turns into a full-blown binge. A binger will typically say things such as:

"I've blown it so I might as well carry on until tomorrow or next week or next month and then start afresh"

"I've eaten three so I might as well eat the whole packet now."

The underlying problem

Just like **anorexia** and **bulimia**, compulsive eating disorder is a way of dealing with deep-rooted unhappiness. It is also a way of coping with the stresses and strains of everyday life. Very often, compulsive eating develops in people with a poor **self-image** and little confidence. It is also possible that many people with compulsive eating disorder eat because they are bored, fed up or lonely.

John

John is a compulsive eater:
'I often wake up in the middle of the night and can't stop thinking about food. I keep thinking about what's in the fridge. If I know there are some leftovers, I just can't get it out of my mind. It's like a battle I can't win. Eventually I just give in. I always do. Then I go and eat the leftovers and usually anything else I can find. Cereals, bread, beans, porridge oats. I just have to keep eating. I just want to fill my mouth with food. When I binge I do not enjoy the food I am eating. Often I don't even taste it. I just have to eat something, anything. Afterwards, I feel disgusted with myself. I want to hide away from the world.'

Who gets eating disorders?

Anyone can develop an **eating disorder** regardless of his or her age, sex, race or background. However there are a number of risk factors that increase the likelihood of an individual developing eating problems. These factors include personality, what happens in their childhood and adolescence and the society in which they live. Research shows that young women, especially between the ages of 15 and 25, are particularly vulnerable to developing eating disorders.

It has also been found that some professions have higher than average rates of eating problems. These include dancing, modelling and horse racing. Many ballet dancers and models talk about the intense pressure they face from their profession, the **media** and their audience to maintain a very slim figure. Many models know they will not get work if they are even slightly overweight. Horse racing jockeys are also constantly under pressure to keep their weight low, leading to claims that illnesses such as **anorexia** and **bulimia** are common amongst professional jockeys.

Who gets anorexia?

Anorexia occurs most commonly in teenage girls and young women, although the number of men suffering from this disorder is increasing. It typically begins at, or just after, **puberty** although it can start at any age and last for many years. Research into anorexia has shown that at least 1 per cent of girls in secondary schools suffer from full-blown anorexia and another 3 per cent have partial **symptoms**.

Some research suggests that certain personality types are more likely to suffer from anorexia, for example, those with a tendency to perfectionism and low **self-esteem**. Some **psychologists** believe that anorexia is more likely to develop in children who are brought up in certain kinds of families. Those who have parents with high expectations of achievement, or parents who are very emotionally involved, appear to be particularly at risk. As are those children who have families who place a lot of emphasis on weight, appearance or food.

A number of professions are believed to contribute to the development of eating disorders. Popstars, models, dancers and horse jockeys are all under pressure to keep their weight down.

Who gets bulimia?

It is not known how widespread this disorder is, but it typically occurs in young women aged 18 years on average. The age of people seeking treatment varies from the early teens to the late sixties and men represent 5 per cent of officially reported cases. **Bulimia** is more commonly found in those girls who attend boarding schools, colleges and universities. One American study revealed a 40 per cent incidence among college women. In some cases bulimia develops from an earlier problem of **anorexia**.

Who gets compulsive eating disorder?

It is thought that more people suffer from this eating disorder than from anorexia and bulimia. Again, although both men and women are affected by it, it is more common in women and it is mostly women who seek help for it.

Men get eating disorders, too

Until recently it was thought that eating disorders were predominantly a 'female illness'. Certainly the statistics supported this belief, with most 'diagnosed' anorexics and bulimics being girls or women. However, over the past few years there has been a rise in the number of reported cases of eating disorders in men. The Eating Disorders Association estimates that approximately 10 per cent of people with eating disorders are men. Like females most male cases start early in life, usually before the age of 15. However, unlike women, many of the men diagnosed with eating disorders also identify themselves as being gay.

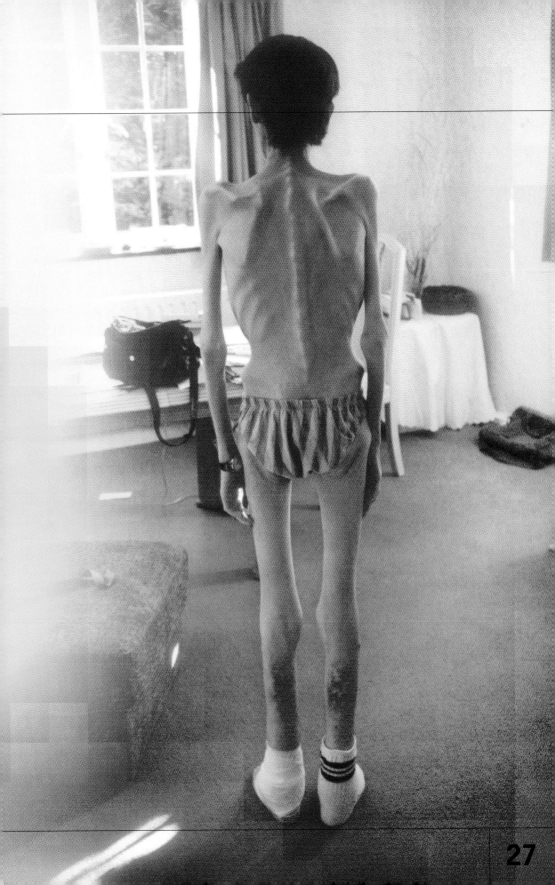

Adolescence

Many of the most serious **eating disorders** affect teenagers and people in their early twenties. So what is it about being a teenager that makes someone more vulnerable to developing eating disorders?

Psychologists who work with young people believe that many of the problems teenagers experience are related to all the changes they have to cope with as they move through adolescence. Some of these changes are with their bodies, some with how other people begin to treat them and others with how young people start to think about themselves and the world.

Physical changes

As young people go through **puberty** their bodies start to change. Boys develop facial hair and their voices become deeper. Girls start menstruating and their bodies change shape and often become more rounded.

For most boys, the changes of puberty are welcome because they make them feel more masculine and confident. For many girls, however, their changing bodies can make them feel overweight and unattractive. Many teenage girls have very poor **self-images**. One of the reasons for this is because many of their **role models**, such as pop stars, television personalities and models, seem to have almost no curves and are very slim. Teenage girls often compare themselves against these role models and feel unattractive.

Adolescence is also a time when young people, particularly girls, are made to feel more conscious of their bodies. At this stage family and friends often begin to make more comments about young women's appearances and these comments can be negative. Boys in particular are prone to making critical comments about girls and their bodies. Such remarks increase a young woman's awareness of her body.

ff Research shows that teasing about body shape and weight is common in schools, and can often precipitate a young person going on a diet.JJ (EDA, 2000)

Adolescence

New demands

At the same time as they develop physically, young people find that there are changes in the way people behave towards them. Families and schoolteachers often expect them to start taking more responsibility for themselves, yet they also often continue to treat them like children. Many parents encourage their children to become more independent but still try to control the clothes their children wear, where and with whom they socialize and their career choices. This treatment can often lead to feelings of conflict and confusion.

As well as demands from parents and teachers, there are also strong pressures on teenagers from friends of the same age. For the first time in their lives it becomes normal for many to have a boyfriend or girlfriend. Within such relationships some degree of sexual contact may be expected. All these expectations can put a lot of pressure on both those who do and those who don't have partners.

Friendships

Young people's **self-esteem** is closely linked to the friends they have. It becomes very important for teenagers to be accepted and liked by their **peer group**. The feedback that a young person gets from this group is often crucial to the way they feel about themselves. Adolescence is a period in which **peer pressure** – to smoke, try drugs, find a boyfriend or girlfriend or have sex – becomes intense. Many people talk about the pain they went through in adolescence, in trying to keep up with their friends or of feeling as if they did not fit in.

❝I really hated school. Every day was just hell. I was so lonely – and everyone knew it. I know people were afraid of being my friend. If they were they would just be seen as being like me, boring, dull, fat and ugly ... the girl with no friends.❞

(Alice)

Although some teenagers seem to sail through adolescence and appear popular, successful and at ease with themselves, far more young people find adolescence a very difficult time. Many of those who develop **eating disorders** experienced problems in their adolescence. Feeling rejected by their peer group appears to be very common in teenagers who do not cope very well with this stage in life.

During adolescence, there can be great pressure to try new 'adult' activities such as drinking alcohol and smoking.

Social pressures

It is widely thought that the society in which people live plays a significant part in the development of **eating disorders**. It is true that in some societies, such as in parts of Africa and Asia, eating disorders hardly exist at all. In Western society it is thought that the importance placed on food and physical appearance, particularly by the **media**, plays a major role in the development of eating disorders.

Society and food

Food is very important in Western society. Everywhere there are places to buy food – fast food take-aways, corner shops, supermarkets, bars and cafes. Eating out is a very popular social activity. Many social events and celebrations have the sharing of food at their heart. It is difficult to escape food wherever you go. We are now encouraged to eat far more than we really need by the advertisements we are constantly exposed to. These messages often urge us to eat for all sorts of reasons other than to satisfy hunger – for relaxation, to enhance our body image or simply because we believe we are getting a bargain. Food is big business.

Mouth-watering images of food are all aimed at whetting our appetites. The images of beautiful people are subtle messages that suggest that by eating this food, we too will look like or be like them.

At the same time as we are encouraged by the media to eat more, we are also told to deny ourselves food. A recipe for chocolate fudge cake in a magazine is likely to be side by side with an article on how to lose weight. The messages that the media are sending out about food and weight are very mixed. It's OK to eat as long as you don't get fat! A difficult balance for anyone to achieve, especially with so much temptation around.

Food also plays a significant role within families. Parents often express their love through the food they provide and prepare for their children. They buy foods as treats and rewards, and often cook 'special meals' that they know their children will like. In some families the only way love can be expressed is through food. So when a bulimic or anorexic child refuses to eat, this is often seen as a rejection of the parent and their love.

Social pressures

Thin is good

Besides bombarding us with powerful and often conflicting messages about food, the **media** also sends out strong messages about how people should look. In the media being slim is seen as part of being happy, attractive, successful, popular and fashionable. Although there is no evidence that happiness is directly related to weight, that is the message that is constantly sent out. These unrealistic messages and images are breeding a society of men and women who find it difficult to accept their bodies as they are, even when they are within a healthy weight range.

Television, magazines and cinema all send out the message that fat is bad, thin is good. This affects the way that people come to think about themselves and others. Overweight people are often the butt of jokes. They find it hard to buy fashionable clothes and can experience **prejudice** in job interviews. Larger people often feel intimidated in communal changing rooms and sports clubs. Not surprisingly, many people become very self-conscious of their size and feel **depressed** and worthless. Such feelings can also affect behaviour. Some people are put off taking up exercise because they feel ashamed in public, while others are driven to **comfort eating** to make up for their feelings of depression and low **self-worth**. However, it is not only overweight people who are affected by the messages about food and body shape that they see all around them. Most people would admit that these messages have influenced them to some degree in their lives.

Women have always been expected to change their shape to suit the fashion of the day. This picture, for example, shows a woman being helped into her corset by a maid. Today, more than at any other time in history, women are expected to be thin.

Emotions

Emotions play a very important part in **eating disorders**. In particular, low **self-esteem** and experiences of stress can lead a young person to develop eating problems.

A variety of childhood experiences can damage a child's developing self-esteem and self-confidence. One of the most important influences on self-esteem is the way children are treated and valued by their parents. Other important experiences come from children's treatment at school and how well their **peer group** accepts them.

Family life

Family life plays a crucial role in the development of self-esteem. Children who are brought up in homes where they are constantly criticized, rejected or given little love and encouragement grow up feeling unlovable and unworthy. Sometimes, eating disorders can be seen as attempts to raise low self-esteem. For example, people with eating disorders typically think, 'if only I became thinner then I would be a better person'. However, just being thinner does not alter a deep-seated sense of poor **self-worth**. Even if anorexics feel slightly better once they have achieved their weight goal, this feeling is likely to be only temporary. Self-esteem cannot be permanently raised by dieting or weight loss. This is tackling the problem at the wrong level. In order to feel really better about themselves, people have to learn to accept and love themselves for who they are.

Comfort

Sometimes binge-eating may begin as a source of comfort for those who lack a warm and loving relationship. In other cases, difficult or unwanted sexual experiences can trigger a crisis in self-confidence that can lead to dieting, **bingeing** and **purging**. For these people sex may be seen as 'disgusting' or 'unpleasant', and may lead to feelings of self-hatred. Often, young people describe their first sexual experience as something they felt they had to do, but when it happened it left them with all sorts of bad feelings about themselves and their bodies. Some of the **symptoms** of eating disorders can be seen as ways of trying to get rid of these feelings or control them.

Difficult challenges, such as exams, and periods of great stress, caused by events like parental divorce or a death in the family, have also been found to trigger eating disorders. Sexual abuse might also be a factor in eating disorders.

"My grandfather died of a terminal illness. After he died I couldn't bear to talk about him to anyone. This feeling of loss grew inside me like a cancer. I went about like a bundle of gloom and would eat and eat and eat."

(Hannah 13)

What are the warning signs?

There are lots of warning signs of **eating disorders**. Although many of the **symptoms** would not, on their own, be a cause for concern – together they may ring alarm bells. Early recognition could prevent the onset of much more serious problems later on.

Anorexia nervosa

The early signs of **anorexia** nervosa are unremarkable and may be confused with some of the normal signs of adolescence. For example, fussiness about food, moodiness, loss of friends and spending increasing time alone. However, as the disorder progresses the signs become more obvious. Weight loss becomes noticeable, as does avoidance of food. An anorexic may take to wearing very baggy clothes to hide their bodies. They may also become very secretive about what they do with their time. Exercising excessively, particularly when dieting, is also a clear sign that a problem exists.

Naturally slim stars, such as Portia de Rossi of *Ally McBeal* fame, provide role models for teenage girls. They themselves can be at the centre of media speculation about eating disorders.

Bulimia nervosa

Bulimia nervosa is harder to spot than anorexia, as the bulimic's weight could be in the normal range. However, after a phase of normal eating, a bulimic may disappear into the bathroom and run water or play the radio loudly to hide the sound of their vomiting. Food often disappears in large amounts and wrappers can be found in unusual places, along with secret stores of food and even packets of **laxatives**. The bulimic may start to spend more time alone and become irritable when disturbed.

Compulsive eating disorder

Compulsive eating disorder is the most difficult eating disorder to recognize. Although many compulsive eaters are overweight, this may not be recognized as a sign of an underlying problem. The compulsive eater may even go up and down in weight just like someone that keeps going on, or coming off, a diet. What is more obvious about the behaviour of compulsive eaters is that they tend to eat secretly or continuously. They also may confess to deep unhappiness about themselves and their eating.

What are the warning signs?

Helping a friend

If you suspect a close friend might be suffering from an **eating disorder**, don't be afraid of raising your concerns with them. It is possible that they are desperate to talk to someone but don't know how to go about it. However, it is important before you do speak to them, that you get some information about eating disorders. At the back of the book are some places that can be contacted for information and advice. You could also make use of your school or local library.

If you feel able to talk to your friend make sure you find a private place to talk. Let them know what you suspect, but also let them know that you are worried and would like to help. Then, give them time to talk and listen carefully to what they say. Don't get angry with them or tell them that they are selfish. Don't tell them that they are silly to feel this way. Instead accept what they say without judging them. It might be that your friend denies that they have a problem. Don't argue with them, because arguing might destroy the trust they have in you.

If your friend agrees that they might have a problem offer to go with them to see a teacher or doctor and wait with them once they have an appointment. Being there for them can be very important.

Remember, whether your friend agrees to get help or not, do not become too involved in their illness. Do not try, for example, to be their rescuer. If help is rejected then do not pressure them to seek help, no matter how difficult it might seem. Remind yourself that you have done what it is reasonable to do. You can still be supportive by listening and being there for them.

Finally, if you do think that the eating disorder is dangerous or life-threatening then you should tell an adult who you think your friend will trust. A teacher, school nurse or youth worker may all be people you could go to.

What families and teachers can do to help

Once a young person accepts help for an **eating disorder** there are a number of things that friends, families and teachers can do to support them through the recovery process. It is important to learn about eating disorders and their treatments. It is crucial that people understand eating disorders are not just about being fussy about food or are just a normal part of growing up. Eating disorders need to be taken seriously and those with them need to be listened to, supported and understood. Parents and teachers need to know that once a young person starts treatment it is unlikely there will be immediate results. Recovery from eating disorders can be very slow and there may be many setbacks along the way. It is important for everyone to be aware of this and continue to be supportive.

Being supportive

Many parents worry about how to manage food and eating when they have a child with an eating disorder. Although it is not easy to strike the right balance, it is important for parents to make their home as supportive as possible without bringing attention to food or their child's problem. This might mean removing scales, diet books and **calorie** counters from view and thinking about what food is bought and where it is kept. Keeping large amounts of cakes, crisps and biscuits in very obvious places might not be very helpful. Mealtimes also need to be kept as relaxed as possible. It is important that parents don't 'police' the amount people eat or try to encourage eating with treats. People also need to remember that 'treats out' at the local pizza parlour or burger bar might be very stressful for an anorexic or bulimic.

Everyone should start to think about the way they speak about others. Many people describe and evaluate others in terms of their appearance and this may have a part to play in the development of eating problems and low **self-esteem**. It is even more important that families, teachers and friends stop themselves from commenting on the appearance of someone with an eating disorder. A comment such as, 'you're looking better now you've put on some weight' might be received with horror by an anorexic. Similarly, if the young person thinks that their weight gain or loss is being monitored by adults this can cause much **anxiety**. The control that they are trying to achieve might be lost.

Helping yourself

You may feel, after reading this book, that you could have an **eating disorder**. First of all if you have any suspicions at all, you must not ignore them. Any disorder, however slight, is much easier to treat in its early stages. There are also a number of things that you can do to help yourself.

Don't bottle things up – talk to someone. It is important that you find someone you can talk to as soon as possible. Choose a person who you think will listen to you. Tell them how you are feeling, that you are worried about yourself and that you think you have a problem. If they just tell you not to worry then they are not the right person to talk to. Try again until you find someone who will take you seriously.

Besides talking over your concerns, you might want to ask for help in finding someone who is qualified to treat people with eating disorders. There are a list of organizations and helplines at the end of the book that you might find useful.

Find out about eating disorders

It is helpful to find out as much as you can about eating disorders. This will not only help you to decide what you have and what you can expect from treatment, but it will also show you that you are not alone. This can be very comforting.

Improve your self-esteem

Poor **self-image** can be at the root of many eating problems. There are a number of things that you can do to help yourself.

Try to accept yourself for who you are. It is natural for bodies to change in adolescence and everybody goes through it. Very few women naturally have rake-like bodies and flat stomachs and few men are born with **six-packs**! Although these shapes have become fashionable, they are impossible for many women and men to achieve.

Your body will change in adolescence but wait until it has settled down before thinking seriously about going on a diet.

Helping yourself

There are lots of things, apart from physical appearance, that make people attractive. Think about the people you like. Do you like them because they are thin or because they are fun, creative or caring? We are all born different, so feel good about your individuality.

Today there are many more different fashions than ever before. Try to find a style that suits you and your personality and that you feel comfortable with. If clothes don't fit you when you try them, don't buy them. If you feel good in what you wear, you are likely to be much more confident.

Weight control

There is a growing tendency for young people to try to lose weight by eating less. However, this can be dangerous at a time when your body is still growing and developing. If you think you really need to lose weight then visit your doctor or school nurse. They will give you advice about the ideal weight for your height and body type, and how to diet healthily.

Extreme dieting is a dangerous way to lose weight. A crash diet may work in the short term but in the long term rapid weight loss is difficult to maintain. **Starvation** decreases the body's rate of using up **calories**, known as the **metabolic rate**. It quickly becomes impossible to keep your weight down on anything but the tiniest intake of food.

Some people have suggested that dieting itself could be a trigger for becoming more **obsessed** with food and eating! One study looked at how a group of soldiers coped with a severe reduction in their food intake. The results were very interesting. For almost half of the men studied, food became the main topic of their conversation, reading and daydreams. Many of the group found it impossible to keep to their diet. They ate secretly and felt guilty afterwards.

Exercise

Exercising is a great way of toning up your body and will also make you feel good in the process. There are lots of really easy ways to exercise. Walk to and from school instead of taking the bus and always chose stairs over lifts. Go swimming, running and dancing. As you feel more confident aim to build three sessions of about 20 minutes exercise into your week.

Controlling what you eat

If you are troubled by **bingeing** there are a number of things you can do to help yourself. Try to make bingeing difficult by throwing away remains of meals or putting snack foods in difficult to reach cupboards. When buying snack foods go for low-**calorie** nibbles. Try to avoid situations where you might eat or buy food just out of habit. For example, avoid walking past the cake shop by taking a different route. Also avoid situations of extreme boredom or hunger. At danger points distract yourself by doing something active.

Sometimes it is useful to keep a record of your progress. Writing things down will help you to identify your successes and also when things go wrong.

Some sufferers of eating disorders find that new interests build up their self-confidence.

In order to gain 1lb (300g) in weight, an additional 3500 calories is required over what is needed to keep weight stable. This is equivalent to the calorific value of 10 chocolate bars or about 45 apples.

Treatment

It is usually very difficult for people with **eating disorders** to get better on their own. However, there are a variety of ways that people can get help for eating disorders. Seeing a doctor can be a good place to start. A doctor will be able to refer a person on to the appropriate services and will also be able to give them information and support.

Once it is confirmed that someone has an eating disorder there are a number of ways in which they might be treated. The treatment will depend upon the type of eating disorder, how severe it is and what is at its roots.

Anorexia nervosa

Anorexia is very hard to treat, partly because it is almost impossible to force someone to eat. However, there could come a stage when the sufferer is so ill that unless they eat, they will die. At this stage, most anorexics go into hospital. Here, the first goal of treatment is to increase and stabilize their weight. Many methods of nourishing anorexics have been tried over the years. Some of these have included force-feeding and confining the patient to bed so that they do not burn up any **calories**. More recently a form of treatment, known as **behaviour therapy**, has been used widely in the treatment of anorexia. This involves encouraging the person to eat by giving privileges for eating and putting on weight and withdrawing them if they do not eat. Privileges include telephone calls, visits and watching television. Some hospital wards also have communal dining areas where all anorexic patients eat together and encourage each other to eat.

Unfortunately, a number of problems have been found with all these treatments. Some patients agree to eat just to get out of hospital. Once they are out they return to their previous habits. Others eat but learn to purge to keep their weight down. Finally, since all these treatments only treat the **symptoms** of the illness, not the cause, they rarely achieve a long-term cure.

These days many treatments try to work with the 'whole problem'. They do this by combining a number of methods that address the immediate problem of low weight but also examine the **psychological** reasons why someone has developed the eating disorder.

In one such treatment an anorexic is asked to keep a diary recording their food intake, their daily activity and their thoughts and feelings. The aim is to encourage the person to reflect on their own behaviour and thinking, and identify how it might influence their eating patterns. The anorexic is asked to give up dieting whilst in treatment and eat regularly and healthily. As the treatment progresses the diaries may reveal that the patient experiences certain moods before eating, or has irrational thoughts about food and weight. The diary might also reveal deeper emotional problems. These issues can then be explored in more detail through therapy. Some people may work with their therapists on the ways they think about food and eating. Others might work on **self-esteem** and others might examine family relationships.

Treatment

Bulimia

People with **bulimia** can return to healthy eating regardless of how long they have been involved with binge eating and **purging**. Furthermore, many of the physical side effects of the illness will disappear in time. The main difficulty for most people is finding a therapist with an adequate training and understanding of this **eating disorder**.

Hospital in-patient treatment will be necessary for only the smallest minority of cases. As with anorexics a range of treatments may be offered. These might include family therapy, diet counselling, group therapy and learning problem-solving skills. Treating the **psychological** aspects of the illness is a very specialized task and often takes the form of therapy. A therapist will develop a relationship with the bulimic and then explore any issues that might be troubling them.

❝I was really lucky to live in an area that had a self-help group for recovering bulimics. It was so good to find out there were other people who had problems just like me. To be able to talk about bingeing and vomiting with people who had been there was such a relief. I didn't feel like a freak anymore. Everyone was so supportive. I also found people I could call on if I was having a bad day. Although I don't think I'll ever feel confident to relax around food, I really feel I am now on the way to getting better.❞

(Zeena)

Compulsive eating disorder

As with **anorexia** and bulimia, it is likely that a person with **compulsive** eating disorder will be offered a range of treatments to help them. Some of the treatment will help them manage their eating and, if they are overweight, lose weight healthily. Other aspects of treatment will try to discover why the person needs to eat and help them work through these problems.

Information and advice

There are a number of organizations that offer support and advice for those wanting to find out more about eating disorders. Most of these organizations will be able to send free information packs and leaflets, and some will be able to answer queries over the telephone. Through many of these organizations you will be able to find details about regional groups and associations in your area.

Contacts in the UK

The Eating Disorders Association
First Floor Wensum House, 103 Prince of Wales Road, Norwich NR1 1DW
Admin: 0870 770 3256
Youth Helpline 01603 765 050 (18 years & under) 4pm to 6.30pm weekdays
e-mail: info@edauk.com
web site: www.edauk.com
The EDA has a range of information leaflets and booklets about eating disorders, some of which are free.

National Youth Agency
17-23 Albion Street, Leicester, LE1 6GD
Tel: 0116 285 3700
e-mail: nya@nya.org.uk
web site: www.nya.org.uk
This is a really useful service. It offers information, support, advice and links for a whole variety of young peoples' issues. It also has a free, and very extensive, library service.

Careline
Tel: 020 8875 0500
e-mail: careline@clara.net
web site: www.careline.org.uk
Confidential telephone counselling for children, young people & adults on any issue. Mon-Fri 10am–8pm, Saturdays 10am–1pm

Overeaters Anonymous
Tel: 07000 784985
web site: www.overeatersanonymous.org

Lighterlife (formerly Obesity lifeline)
Tel: 0870 664747
e-mail: inform@lighterlife.co.uk
web site: www.obesitylifeline.co.uk

Contacts in Australia

Anorexia Bulimia Nervosa Associations Inc.
First Floor – Woodards House, 47-49 Waymouth Street, Adelaide, SA 5000
Tel: 61 8 8212 1644 Fax: 61 8 8212 7991
e-mail: mail@abnasa.asn.au
web site: www.span.com.au/anorexia

Eating Disorders Support Network Inc. (NSW)
PO Box 532, Willoughby NSW 2068
Support and Information Line: 61 2 9412 4499
e-mail: edsn@edsn.asn.au
web site: www.edsn.asn.au

Eating Disorders Association Inc. (Queensland)
PO Box 138, Wilston, Queensland, 4051
e-mail: eda.inc@uq.net.au
web site: www.uq.net.au/eda

Eating Disorders Foundation of Victoria
513 High Street, Glen Iris, Victoria 3146
Tel: (03) 9885 0318 Fax: (03) 9885 1153
e-mail: edfv@eatingdisorders.org.au
web site: www.eatingdisorders.org.au

Further reading

Here are some books that you might like to read
for further advice and information.

Anorexia Nervosa: The Wish to Change
by Crisp, Joughin, Halek & Bowyer
Psychology Press, 1996

Finding Out ... About Eating Disorders
Hobsons Academic Relations, 1999

**Wise Guides – Eating (Improve
Your Body Image)**
by Anita Naik, Hodder Children's Books, 1999

The Best Little Girl in the World
by Levenkron, Puffin Books, 1996
This is a novel about a young girl who becomes
increasingly unhappy with herself and feels that
the solution is to lose weight. It is an interesting
read for anyone who wants to gain a better
understanding of the emotions and feelings that
can arise while suffering from an eating disorder.

Glossary

anorexia
(also anorexia nervosa) lack of appetite for food. An emotional disorder involving an obsessive desire to lose weight by refusing to eat. A person who suffers from anorexia is known as an 'anorexic'.

anxiety
feeling worried

behaviour therapy
form of therapy that concentrates on changing the behaviour of the patient, often through the use of rewards.

bingeing
eating large amounts of food at one time

bulimia
(also bulimia nervosa) an emotional disorder involving overeating, usually alternating with fasting or self-induced vomiting or purging. A person who suffers from bulimia is known as a 'bulimic'.

calorie
unit for measuring the energy value of food

comfort eating
eating to make oneself feel less anxious or worried

compulsive
overwhelming urge to do something

constipation
difficulty in going to the toilet

dehydration
lacking water or fluid in the body, which causes many side effects

depression
severe unhappiness, especially when long-lasting

distorted
twisted out of shape – unreal

distress
extreme anxiety

eating disorder
medical condition in which people either under-eat (anorexia) or over-eat and fast or deliberately vomit (bulimia), usually caused by a psychological fear of weight gain or an obsession with food

fasting
deliberately going without food

incontinence
problem in controlling bowel or bladder movements

laxatives
tablets that stop the digestion of food and make people go to the toilet

media
magazines, newspapers, television and films

metabolic rate
rate at which your body uses up food

obese
weighing more than 20 per cent above normal requirements for one's height and skeletal structure

obsession
thought that won't go away and seems uncontrollable

osteoporosis
medical condition in which the bones become brittle or fragile, usually due to a deficiency of calcium or vitamin D

peer group
group of people who are all the same age

peer pressure
pressure from people of the same age to behave in a certain way

prejudice
unreasonable opinion of someone or something

psychological
relating to the mind and behaviour

psychologist
someone who has trained to work with and understand people

puberty
period of time when teenagers experience changes in their bodies

purging
getting rid of food that has been eaten or digested by vomiting or taking laxatives

remorse
feeling guilty or sorry

role model
someone who is admired and copied

rituals
behaviours that are carried out in regular, routine ways – such as always preparing food in the same way or eating it in the same order

salivary glands
place in the body where saliva is made

self-esteem
opinion that someone has of herself or himself

self-image
way someone sees herself or himself

self-worth
way someone feels about, or values, herself or himself

six-pack
common term for a set of well-developed abdominal muscles

starvation
deprived of food – sometimes to the point of death

stigma
being seen as different

symptoms
signs of an illness

Index